THE FUTURE IS FEMALE

ALTERNATOR BOOKS™

Changemakers in

SPACE

Women Leading the Way

CROWN SHEPHERD

Lerner Publications ◆ Minneapolis

Always reach for the stars

Lerner Publications Company
An imprint of Lerner Publishing Group, Inc.
241 First Avenue North
Minneapolis, MN 55401 USA

For reading levels and more information, look up this title at www.lernerbooks.com.

Main body text set in Aptifer Sans LT Pro Medium.
Typeface provided by Linotype AG.

Designer: Athena Currier
Lerner team: Martha Kranes

Library of Congress Cataloging-in-Publication Data

Names: Shepherd, Crown, author.
Title: Changemakers in space : women leading the way / Crown Shepherd.
Description: Minneapolis : Lerner Publications, [2024] | Series: The future is female (Alternator Books) | Includes bibliographical references and index. | Audience: Ages 8–12 | Audience: Grades 4–6 | Summary: "Readers blast off on an exciting adventure in this book about the women who defined space travel. They'll discover the changemakers who created new technology, piloted spacecraft, and much more"— Provided by publisher.
Identifiers: LCCN 2023028845 (print) | LCCN 2023028846 (ebook) | ISBN 9798765608883 (library binding) | ISBN 9798765625026 (paperback) | ISBN 9798765618387 (epub)
Subjects: LCSH: Women astronauts—Biography—Juvenile literature. | Astronauts—Biography—Juvenile literature. | Women atronomers—Biography—Juvenile literature. | Astronomers—Biography—Juvenile literature. | BISAC: JUVENILE NONFICTION / Biography & Autobiography / Women
Classification: LCC TL789.85.A1 S54 2024 (print) | LCC TL789.85.A1 (ebook) | DDC 629.4500922—dc23/eng/20230711

LC record available at https://lccn.loc.gov/2023028845
LC ebook record available at https://lccn.loc.gov/2023028846

Manufactured in the United States of America
1-1009550-51566-6/13/2023

Table of Contents

INTRODUCTION

Take off

On July 16, 1969, Apollo 11 blasted off the ground. Traveling thousands of miles per hour, it headed into space. Days later, it became the first spacecraft to land on the moon. A mathematician, Katherine Johnson, helped make this possible.

The only Black woman working on an otherwise all-white and male team, Johnson changed space travel forever. Her calculations helped to put the first humans on the moon with Apollo 11. Johnson had worked on calculations behind the trip to the moon for years. She helped figure out how

Johnson calculated spacecrafts' flights.

to get a spacecraft into the moon's orbit, what part of the moon would make a safe landing place, how to get the astronauts home safely, and much more.

From Mary Jackson, the first Black woman engineer at the National Aeronautics and Space Administration (NASA), to Kitty O'Brien Joyner, the first female engineer at the National Advisory Committee for Aeronautics (NACA), women have pushed the boundaries of space exploration. Not every woman who has contributed to space can be included in this book. But the women on these these pages have changed what we know about space and how we get there.

CHAPTER 1

Making History

Women have shaped space travel. Women in this chapter were firsts in their fields. But they made sure they weren't the last.

The Human Computer

Dorothy Vaughan was a high school math teacher. Later, she left teaching to become a mathematician for NACA. The agency researched and did experiments on planes. In 1949 Vaughan supervised a group of "human computers," or people who were able to easily do advanced calculations. NACA

Vaughan was a manager at NASA for ten years.

was replaced by NASA in 1958. Vaughan became an expert programmer and NASA's first Black manager. She contributed to several space projects. Throughout her career, Vaughan helped other women in their own careers.

Paving the Way

Nicole Mann, a member of the Round Valley Indian Tribes, was a marine pilot and flew large planes. She joined NASA's astronaut class in 2013. In October 2022, Mann boarded the

Dragon spacecraft and traveled to space. She became the first Native American woman in space. On her first trip, Mann brought a dream catcher from her mother.

Mann aboard the International Space Station (ISS)

OUT OF THIS WORLD

In 1983 Sally Ride was the first US woman in space. She helped launch and retrieve satellites.

Ride went into space two different times.

piloting the Skies

Growing up, Eileen Collins knew she wanted to be a pilot. She joined the air force in 1979 as a pilot and as a math and flight instructor. She became an astronaut in 1990.

Collins looking over notes on the Discovery shuttle in 1995

Collins later made history by becoming the first woman to fly and command a space shuttle. She piloted the Discovery on an eight-day mission. Collins spent over 6,751 hours in space on thirty different types of aircraft.

"I wanted to be part of our nation's space program. It's the greatest adventure on this planet—or off the planet, for that matter. I wanted to fly the Space Shuttle."

—EILEEN COLLINS

Never Give Up

Ellen Ochoa applied to NASA's astronaut program three times before being accepted in 1990. She went to space for the first time in 1993. That space trip made her the first Latina in space. Ochoa was a mission specialist in charge of launching a satellite into space. She went into space four times before becoming the first Latinx director of the Johnson Space Center. It is NASA's center for human spaceflight.

Ochoa aboard a spacecraft in 2002

The Icebuster

Judith Resnik was the first Jewish woman in space. Resnik joined NASA in 1978. She flew to space for the first time in 1984. She was a mission specialist on the space shuttle Discovery. She spent over 144 hours in space. While in space, Resnik and other astronauts removed ice from their spacecraft. This earned her crew the nickname Icebusters. In 1986 Resnik was ready to go into space again. But the space shuttle Challenger took off and soon exploded. Resnik and the crew died. People still celebrate Resnik and her work.

Resnik was a NASA astronaut and engineer.

FLYING HIGH

Liu Yang (*below*) is the first Chinese woman to travel into space. She joined China's army and learned how to fly planes. She flew cargo planes for the army. In 2010 she joined the astronaut corps. Two years later, she flew to space and made history. Yang spent six months in space and was in charge of medical experiments.

Leading from Space

Astronaut Kalpana Chawla was born in India. She immigrated to the US in the 1980s. She flew on her first spaceflight in 1997. She is the first woman from India to travel into space.

Chawla went into space a second time aboard space shuttle Columbia. On that spaceflight she conducted about eighty experiments with her crew members. The shuttle exploded in 2003 while returning to Earth. Chawla and her crew died. People continue to honor her, her accomplishments, and those of the other crew members.

Chawla reviews a checklist on the Columbia space shuttle in 2003.

COMMANDING A SPACE STATION

In 2007 Peggy Whitson made history by becoming the first female commander of the ISS.

Whitson was the first woman to command the ISS twice.

CHAPTER 2

Looking Up

The night sky helps us learn more about space. These women are looking up and changing the world's understanding of space.

Making Discoveries

Carolyn Shoemaker was a high school teacher and mother of three. At the age of fifty-one, she decided to become an astronomer. Shoemaker discovered over eight hundred asteroids and thirty-two comets. She set a record for the most astronomical discoveries. Parenting sharpened her attention to detail and patience. These qualities helped her make so many discoveries. In 1993, at the age of sixty-four, Shoemaker codiscovered Comet Shoemaker-Levy 9. The discovery of this comet changed the way scientists thought about comets and the planet Jupiter.

Shoemaker (*right*) and the astronomers with whom she codiscovered Comet Shoemaker-Levy 9

Changing Astronomy

Andrea Ghez is an astronomer studying black holes. These areas have so much gravity that nothing can escape from them—not even light. After twenty-five years of research, Ghez discovered a supermassive black hole in the center of the Milky Way. Her discovery won her the Nobel Prize in Physics.

Ghez gives a talk in 2013.

> "Remember that outstanding people do not become great overnight. They have to keep focus until they become victors in their mission."
>
> —WANDA DÍAZ-MERCED

An illustration of a black hole

Listening to Space

Since childhood, Wanda Díaz-Merced loved space. She studied space in college. But she had a condition that caused her to lose her sight. She wasn't sure if she could have a career in space. Then a classmate had her listen to a live recording of the sounds of space. People had used sound to study space before. Díaz-Merced built software that let people study space through sound. Her research helped scientists to find black holes more easily than they could using sight.

MOTHER OF HUBBLE

Nancy Roman was the first NASA chief of astronomy. In the 1950s and 1960s, she broke barriers for women within the science community. She created and led a team of astronomers and engineers to make the Hubble. It is the largest telescope orbiting Earth.

Roman with a model of a satellite in 1962

Bouman after speaking about her work helping create the first image of a black hole

The Computer Scientist

Katie Bouman is a computer scientist. She didn't know anything about black holes when she joined a project studying them in 2013. Bouman studied data from telescopes. Then she developed equations to understand the information. In 2019 Bouman, with a team of scientists, used her equations to create the first picture of a black hole.

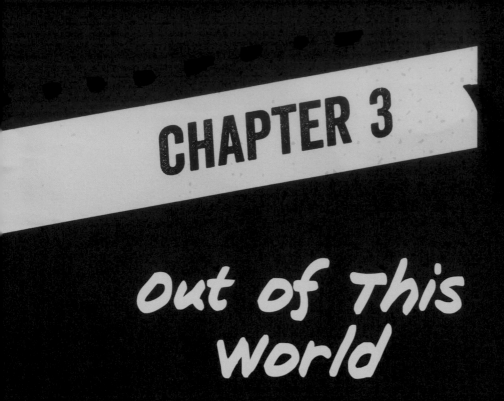

CHAPTER 3

Out of This World

Astronauts in this chapter have flown into space and broken records along the way.

Space and the Body

Jessica Meir spent years studying animals in different environments before she started working for NASA in 2000. Meir joined NASA to study the way the body reacted in space. She started astronaut training in 2013. Meir flew into space and studied how the heart acts in space. She was a part of the history-making first all-female space walk team. They swapped a battery unit on the outer part of the ISS.

On her two trips at the ISS, Williams completed four space walks.

New Record

Sunita Williams loved to fly. She flew several aircraft in the navy. She joined NASA in 1998 and first flew into space in 2006. She was back in space six years later with another trip to the ISS. During her time at the ISS, Williams conducted research, made repairs, and installed a camera on a robotic arm. Williams took seven space walks and logged more than fifty hours in a space suit. She set the record in 2006 for most space walks by a woman. Her record was later broken by Peggy Whitson.

Koch works with robots in 2019.

To the Moon

Christina Koch had several jobs at NASA before becoming an astronaut in 2013. Koch completed six space walks. On these space walks, she conducted hundreds of experiments and made repairs to equipment. In 2019 Koch made history twice. She was a part of the first all-woman space walk in history. And she spent 328 Earth days in space—the longest single spaceflight by a woman. Koch is slated to become the first woman to fly around the moon in the Artemis II moon mission.

Dreaming Big

When she was a little girl, Jessica Watkins dreamed about going to space. She even wrote a poem, "My Little Astronaut," about her imagined adventures in space. Her dreams came true in 2022. Watkins traveled to the ISS. She was the first Black woman to live and work on the space station. She experimented with how to grow food in space. She also broke the record for the longest a Black woman had been in space.

Watkins participates in an experiment on the ISS in 2022.

WOMEN IN SPACE

In 1963 Valentina Tereshkova became the first woman in space. As of March 2023, seventy-eight women have flown in space.

Trereshkova spent seventy-one hours in space in 1963.

Engineering from Space

Stephanie Wilson fell in love with astronomy and engineering as a teenager and became an engineer. Wilson is the second Black woman to travel to space. She was a mission specialist in charge of operating the robotic arm for three space missions. She won a NASA Space Flight Medal for each of these missions. It is awarded for great service during a spaceflight mission.

Wilson received NASA's Distinguished Service Medal two times.

A Step for All Women

Svetlana Savitskaya made history on July 25, 1984, as the first woman to walk in space. In three hours and thirty-five minutes, she did several tasks in space, including testing a new space tool.

CONCLUSION

Reach for the Stars

Women have been making huge contributions to space. They have put people on the moon, walked in space, and discovered distant comets. Those contributions have changed the way we see space and the stars. You can be a part of space history too. In school you can learn more about science, technology, engineering, and math. These areas all help astronauts and astronomers know more about space. You can also read books about space. And at night, you can look up at the sky and see what you notice.

You can start studying space by looking up at the sky.

Glossary

asteroid: a small, rocky object in outer space that goes around the sun

astronaut: someone who travels in a spacecraft into outer space

astronomer: someone who studies stars, planets, and other objects in outer space

comet: an object in outer space that develops a long, bright tail when it passes near the sun

dream catcher: a circular framed net with a hole in the center that is used by some Native Americans to help block bad dreams and catch good ones

experiment: a test done under controlled conditions to learn about something

mathematician: an expert in math

spacecraft: a vehicle for traveling in outer space

spaceflight: a flight into outer space in a vehicle

supervise: to be in charge of someone or something

telescope: a device that helps people see things that are far away

Source Notes

8   Ari Shapiro, Taylor Hutchison, and Patrick Jarenwattananon, "Nicole Mann Will Be the 1st Native Women in Space," NPR, August 22, 2022, https://www.npr.org/2022/08/22/1118843610/nicole-mann-will-be -the-1st-native-woman-in-space.

10   "Eileen Collins—NASA's First Female Shuttle Commander to Lead Next Shuttle Mission," NASA, October 4, 2003, https://www.nasa.gov/vision/space/preparingtravel/Eileen_Collins.html.

19   "Wanda Díaz-Merced," Royal Society, accessed April 20, 2023, https://royalsociety.org/topics-policy/diversity-in-science/scientists-with-disabilities/wanda-diaz-merced/.

Learn More

Britannica Kids: Nicole Aunapu Mann
https://kids.britannica.com/kids/article/Nicole-Aunapu-Mann/634977

Hansen, Grace. *Katherine Johnson: NASA Mathematician*. Minneapolis: Pop!, 2023.

Loh-Hagan, Virginia. *Kalpana Chawla*. Ann Arbor, MI: Cherry Lake, 2023.

National Geographic Kids: Passport to Space
https://kids.nationalgeographic.com/space

Parkin, Michelle. *Ellen Ochoa*. Chicago: Norwood House, 2023.

Time for Kids: A Day in Space
https://www.timeforkids.com/g2/a-day-in-space/?rl=en-490

Time for Kids: 10 Questions for Jessica Watkins
https://www.timeforkids.com/g34/10-q-jessica-watkins/

Tyner, Dr. Artika R. *Changemakers in STEM: Women Leading the Way*. Minneapolis: Lerner Publications, 2024.

Index

Photo Acknowledgments

Images used: NASA, pp. 5, 7, 8, 9, 10, 11, 12, 15, 20, 23, 24, 25; Manfred Werner/
Wikimedia Commons (CC BY-SA 3.0), p. 13; NASA/Getty Images, p. 14; AP Photo, p. 17;
Stefanie Keenan/Getty Images, p. 18; Vadim Sadovski/Shutterstock, p. 19; JOSE LUIS
MAGANA/AFP/Getty Images, p .21; Sovfoto/Universal Images Group/Getty Images,
p. 26; NASA/Bill Ingalls, p. 27; AstroStar/Shutterstock, p. 29. Design elements: Old
Man Stocker/Shutterstock; MPFphotography/Shutterstock; schab/Shutterstock.

Cover: AP Photo/Josh Valcarcel/NASA; Paul Hennessy/Anadolu Agency/Getty Images;
NASA.